When Emily Jones was given her grandmother's medallion, she had no idea it would change her life forever. As she walked into her grandmother's garden, the gem on the medallion started to glow brighter and brighter, and when she reached a giant tree, a circle of blue light appeared. Emily was amazed. What was it? Could it be a portal? She had to take a look and see. And that is how her magical journey began . . .

An Enchanted Land

The world spun around and suddenly Emily found herself in a land she had never seen before. Everything looked so strange and new. She was fascinated by the brightly coloured flowers and sparkling blue water.

'Who are you?' asked a strange, cheerful voice.

Emily turned to see a beautiful girl with pointy ears and flaming-red hair.

'I'm Emily Jones,' she replied. 'Who are you?'

'I'm Azari, a Fire Elf. Welcome to our Elven world.'

'Elven-what? Your ears aren't real, are they? Elves only exist in fairy tales!' Emily was stunned. What was going on?

'How did you get here?' the Fire Elf asked.

'From there!' Emily pointed at the tree, but now it just looked like any other tree. 'I came out of it somehow . . . and I don't know how to go back!'

'We should go and see Farran, the Earth Elf,' Azari suggested. 'He knows everything about trees.'

Hesitantly, Emily followed. Azari talked the whole way, but Emily was too amazed by the beauty of the new world to pay much attention.

Finally, they reached a tree house.

'Farran!' Azari called. A green-eyed elf popped his head out of one of the windows, and hurried down to join them.

'This is Emily Jones. She came here through a tree, and now we need to get her home,' Azari explained.

'Hi Emily! Nice to . . . wow! Your tiny ears aren't real, are they?!' Farran grinned, peering at them curiously.

Before Emily could answer, someone else arrived – Aira, a Wind Elf!

'I couldn't help overhearing,' said Aira. She had a mysterious expression on her face. 'And, Emily, I think I can help. I know a legend about a portal.'

So they all gathered inside Farran's house and Aira began her story.

'The legend says that there were once five sisters. Four of them were Elves and belonged to different elements, but the fifth one wasn't magical and moved to a different world. The Elves created a portal so she could return to the Elven world whenever she liked. Four keys were used to open the portal and protect it from unwanted guests. Unfortunately, the fifth sister became mortal. She grew old and couldn't visit any more. Without her, the sisters drifted apart and never saw each other again.'

'Wow,' Farran breathed. 'I think we need to find those keys to get Emily home. Naida can probably help!'

'Naida's a Water Elf,' Azari explained. 'And she might have a map to help us find the keys.'

Elves? Legends? Keys? Maps? Emily had no idea what was going on . . . but she couldn't wait for the adventure to start!

Emily's Elven Friends

Emily's four new friends are very special.
Each one was born with a different elemental power . . .

Aira

Aira Windwhistler – Wind Elf

Aira is happy, hyperactive, confident and very good at solving problems. Although she is isn't terribly musical, she loves to sing. Aira has power over the wind and many friends among the flying creatures.

Azari

Azari Firedancer – Fire Elf

Azari is spontaneous, cheerful and full of energy. She hates being bored and sometimes acts before she thinks. She can control fire . . . as much as fire can be controlled, that is!

Farran

Farran Leafshade – Earth Elf

Sensible, calm and reliable, Farran is
a really good friend. He sees himself
as a leader, but tends to overthink
things and get insecure. He can
communicate with animals
and plants.

Naida

Naida Riverheart – Water Elf

A dreamer who follows her heart,
Naida is smart, caring and
compassionate. She can control
water and has a special relationship
with aquatic animals.

Magic Bracelet

Use your special mini-set to create your very own elements bracelet!
Follow the illustrated steps to make your bracelet and slip it on
your wrist when it is finished. Can you feel the magic?

Now you're ready to solve puzzles and find
the four keys that will unlock the portal.

During your magical journey, look out for the pages with
gemstones next to the page number, and see how many
element symbols you can spot on each page. Circle the ones
you spot and use your bracelet to help you correctly
identify the symbols.

Mysterious Land

First, try cracking this secret Elf code to discover where Emily found herself when she travelled through the magic portal.

Special Symbols

These element symbols aren't quite finished. Look carefully at the special symbols on your bracelet, then use your felt-tip pens to make the ones on the page match them exactly!

Elemental Powers

Use your imagination to design your own symbols for each of the elements. You'll need one for Fire, Water, Air and Earth.

Welcome to Elvendale

The four keys Emily is looking for are hidden
all over Elvendale. As you find each key, make sure
to mark its location on this map.

Lava Field

This place is hot! Tropical flowers
and fiery animals live here. It's also
famous for its lava bakery, which serves
delicious cinnamon buns! Yummy!

Sparkle Rock

Made from diamonds, Sparkle Rock
shines beautifully over Elvendale in
the sun. It has lots of secret caves
filled with gemstones.

Leaf Land

A green and lush forest, Leaf Land is
home to magical animals and stunning
flowers. It's also where Farran, Naida,
Azari and Aira live.

Desertlands

Sparkle
Rock

Highland

Fores

Sky Castle

This stunning castle sits on top of the highest mountain in the Actan mountain range. It is home to Skyra the Sky Queen, the guardian of a magic portal to the human world. Nobody has visited the castle in many years, and it is said to be cursed by an evil spell.

The great mountain of Silad

Ivy Beach

Blue Water Bay

Lava field

Venti High Hill

Leaf land

yan

The Izdur Ocean

Enki Island

Venti High Hill

From here you can see over most of Elvendale! Venti High Hill is Aira's favourite place, and she has her workshop here.

The Izdur Ocean

Izdur's waters stretch all the way to Enki Island out on the horizon. It's a great place for fantastic, adventure-filled voyages.

The land of
Elvendale

Written in the Stars

The sky over Elvendale is lit by millions of stars! Look above and join the dots to find the constellation that looks like a wave – the symbol of Naida, the Water Elf. The water is where your search for the keys begins!

Upon the Lake

As you sail off on Naida's Adventure Ship to find the first key,
can you spot twelve differences between the ship and
its reflection in the water?

Whirlpool Wonder

Help Naida find her way through the whirlpool
to reach the key at the bottom of the Izdur Ocean.
Be careful not to walk on white!

Mystery Location

Nice work, you found the first key!
If you want to find the next one, you'll need to solve
an ancient riddle, then mark the spot on Naida's map.

Desertlands

Red Mountain

The great mountain of Silad

Sparkle Rock

Ivy Beach

Blue Water Bay

The Izduro Ocean

Enki Island

Love Field

Kenti High Hill

Leaf land

Highland of Helyan

Forest of Deep Secrets

To look for the key
you must be spritely,
and start where lots of
rocks shine brightly.

A Cunning Plan

Well done, you found the right place on the map!
This little squirrel is guarding the second key. Someone has
to catch her, but who? Follow the twisting paths to find out.

Gemstone Puzzle

The squirrel will only let you have the key if you rebuild
her house. Help her out by choosing the right
gemstones to fill the spaces.

A Delicious Challenge

The map leads the friends to a lava bakery in the forest, packed full of yummy treats! Can you help them spot ten pink cupcakes in the picture? Then help look for the third key!

Firefox Shadows

Flamy is no ordinary fox – he's a firefox and he lives by the lava bakery.
Can you circle the shadow that matches him exactly?

Time to Fly

Aira has made some wonderful wings in her workshop on Venti
High Hill. Try designing your own pair, so you can fly high to find
the fourth key. You can decorate them with whatever you like – the sky's
the limit!

Up, Up and Away!

A gust of wind has scattered these element symbols.
Can you put them back in the right places? Remember that each
symbol can only be used once in each row, column and 4x4 square.

Flying Creature

Follow the guide below to colour in this picture.
When you've finished, you'll know where the fourth key is!
Now that you have all four magic keys, you must fly
to Skyra's magic castle . . .

Powers Unite!

Help the friends to reach the magic portal.
Remember that they need to go through all the doors, even those that
lead to the outside, and that they can go through each door only once.

START

Time for your last challenge!
Which chamber door did each Elf
use their powers to open?
Write the letters in the correct
circles and get ready to meet Skyra . . .

FINISH

A

B

C

D

Which Element Are You?

Answer these questions to find out which element
and Elf you most identify with.

1) When I close my eyes and imagine a wonderful place, I see . . .

- a volcano erupting
- a fantastic view from the highest mountaintop
- coral reefs at the bottom of the ocean
- lush rainforest in the jungle

2) If I could, I would colour the world . . .

 green   blue   red   purple

3) My trip of a lifetime would be . . .

- flying up in the clouds
- hiking in the forest
- sailing on waves
- travelling to another galaxy

4) I would describe myself as . . .

- happy and hyperactive
- sensitive and wise
- responsible and helpful
- spontaneous and optimistic

5) The animal that fascinates me the most is . . .

 a dolphin   a fox   a cougar   a bird

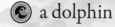

WHICH SYMBOL
DID YOU PICK THE MOST?

You are as spontaneous, brave and funny as Azari.
You love to be the centre of attention. You're fun-loving and
it's impossible to get bored with you!

You are sensible and reliable like Farran. You don't like
change, and you become strongly attached to people.
It makes you a devoted friend.

You love daydreaming and are not afraid to trust your
intuition, just like Naida. You are sensitive and empathetic,
so you like helping others. No wonder you have so many friends!

You are bright, curious and know a lot of
interesting facts! You are super quick at solving
all sorts of problems, just like Aira.

Answers

Page 9

Page 10

Pages 14–15

Pages 16–17

Pages 18–19

Pages 20–21

Page 22

Pages 24–25

Pages 26–27